HOMEBREWER'S
NOTEBOOK

Homebrewer's Notebook
2nd Edition
© 2013 by Michele Costello
ISBN 978-1493555406

As technology advances, it reverses the characteristics of every situation again and again. The age of automation is going to be the age of "do it yourself".

—Marshall McLuhan

TABLE OF CONTENTS

	Beer Name	Style	Date
#1			
#2			
#3			
#4			
#5			
#6			
#7			
#8			
#9			
#10			
#11			
#12			
#13			
#14			
#15			
#16			
#17			
#18			
#19			
#20			
#21			
#22			
#23			
#24			
#25			

	Beer Name	Style	Date
#26			
#27			
#28			
#29			
#30			
#31			
#32			
#33			
#34			
#35			
#36			
#37			
#38			
#39			
#40			
#41			
#42			
#43			
#44			
#45			
#46			
#47			
#48			
#49			
#50			

|

Style				Color	SRM
Recipe Type	Malt Extract	Partial	All Grain	Bitterness	IBU / EBU
Yield				% Alcohol	ABV / ABW
Start Date					

Ingredients

[Circle One]	Amount	Type	Notes
Grains Hops Yeast Malt Extract Other			
Grains Hops Yeast Malt Extract Other			
Grains Hops Yeast Malt Extract Other			
Grains Hops Yeast Malt Extract Other			
Grains Hops Yeast Malt Extract Other			
Grains Hops Yeast Malt Extract Other			
Grains Hops Yeast Malt Extract Other			
Grains Hops Yeast Malt Extract Other			
Grains Hops Yeast Malt Extract Other			
Grains Hops Yeast Malt Extract Other			
Grains Hops Yeast Malt Extract Other			
Grains Hops Yeast Malt Extract Other			
Grains Hops Yeast Malt Extract Other			
Grains Hops Yeast Malt Extract Other			
Grains Hops Yeast Malt Extract Other			
Grains Hops Yeast Malt Extract Other			
Grains Hops Yeast Malt Extract Other			
Grains Hops Yeast Malt Extract Other			

Brewing Notes

Fermentation Notes

Yeast Pitching Temperature			°F / C
Original Gravity			
Primary Fermentation		days	°F / C
Secondary Fermentation		days	°F / C
Final Gravity			

Bottling Notes | Date

Tasting Notes

Date	Rating	Description

2

Style		Color	SRM
Recipe Type	Malt Extract Partial All Grain	Bitterness	IBU / EBU
Yield		% Alcohol	ABV / ABW
Start Date			

Ingredients

[Circle One]	Amount	Type	Notes
Grains Hops Yeast Malt Extract Other			
Grains Hops Yeast Malt Extract Other			
Grains Hops Yeast Malt Extract Other			
Grains Hops Yeast Malt Extract Other			
Grains Hops Yeast Malt Extract Other			
Grains Hops Yeast Malt Extract Other			
Grains Hops Yeast Malt Extract Other			
Grains Hops Yeast Malt Extract Other			
Grains Hops Yeast Malt Extract Other			
Grains Hops Yeast Malt Extract Other			
Grains Hops Yeast Malt Extract Other			
Grains Hops Yeast Malt Extract Other			
Grains Hops Yeast Malt Extract Other			
Grains Hops Yeast Malt Extract Other			
Grains Hops Yeast Malt Extract Other			
Grains Hops Yeast Malt Extract Other			
Grains Hops Yeast Malt Extract Other			
Grains Hops Yeast Malt Extract Other			

Brewing Notes

Fermentation Notes

Yeast Pitching Temperature		°F / C
Original Gravity		
Primary Fermentation	days	°F / C
Secondary Fermentation	days	°F / C
Final Gravity		

Bottling Notes | Date

Tasting Notes

Date	Rating	Description

3

Style				Color	SRM
Recipe Type	Malt Extract	Partial	All Grain	Bitterness	IBU / EBU
Yield				% Alcohol	ABV / ABW
Start Date					

Ingredients

[Circle One]	Amount	Type	Notes
Grains Hops Yeast Malt Extract Other			
Grains Hops Yeast Malt Extract Other			
Grains Hops Yeast Malt Extract Other			
Grains Hops Yeast Malt Extract Other			
Grains Hops Yeast Malt Extract Other			
Grains Hops Yeast Malt Extract Other			
Grains Hops Yeast Malt Extract Other			
Grains Hops Yeast Malt Extract Other			
Grains Hops Yeast Malt Extract Other			
Grains Hops Yeast Malt Extract Other			
Grains Hops Yeast Malt Extract Other			
Grains Hops Yeast Malt Extract Other			
Grains Hops Yeast Malt Extract Other			
Grains Hops Yeast Malt Extract Other			
Grains Hops Yeast Malt Extract Other			
Grains Hops Yeast Malt Extract Other			
Grains Hops Yeast Malt Extract Other			
Grains Hops Yeast Malt Extract Other			

Brewing Notes

Fermentation Notes

Yeast Pitching Temperature		°F / C
Original Gravity		
Primary Fermentation	days	°F / C
Secondary Fermentation	days	°F / C
Final Gravity		

Bottling Notes | Date

Tasting Notes

Date	Rating	Description

4

Style		Color	SRM
Recipe Type	Malt Extract Partial All Grain	Bitterness	IBU / EBU
Yield		% Alcohol	ABV / ABW
Start Date			

Ingredients

[Circle One]	Amount	Type	Notes
Grains Hops Yeast Malt Extract Other			
Grains Hops Yeast Malt Extract Other			
Grains Hops Yeast Malt Extract Other			
Grains Hops Yeast Malt Extract Other			
Grains Hops Yeast Malt Extract Other			
Grains Hops Yeast Malt Extract Other			
Grains Hops Yeast Malt Extract Other			
Grains Hops Yeast Malt Extract Other			
Grains Hops Yeast Malt Extract Other			
Grains Hops Yeast Malt Extract Other			
Grains Hops Yeast Malt Extract Other			
Grains Hops Yeast Malt Extract Other			
Grains Hops Yeast Malt Extract Other			
Grains Hops Yeast Malt Extract Other			
Grains Hops Yeast Malt Extract Other			
Grains Hops Yeast Malt Extract Other			
Grains Hops Yeast Malt Extract Other			

Brewing Notes

Fermentation Notes

Yeast Pitching Temperature			°F / C
Original Gravity			
Primary Fermentation		days	°F / C
Secondary Fermentation		days	°F / C
Final Gravity			

Bottling Notes | Date

Tasting Notes

Date	Rating	Description

5

Style		Color	SRM
Recipe Type	Malt Extract Partial All Grain	Bitterness	IBU / EBU
Yield		% Alcohol	ABV / ABW
Start Date			

Ingredients

[Circle One]	Amount	Type	Notes
Grains Hops Yeast Malt Extract Other			
Grains Hops Yeast Malt Extract Other			
Grains Hops Yeast Malt Extract Other			
Grains Hops Yeast Malt Extract Other			
Grains Hops Yeast Malt Extract Other			
Grains Hops Yeast Malt Extract Other			
Grains Hops Yeast Malt Extract Other			
Grains Hops Yeast Malt Extract Other			
Grains Hops Yeast Malt Extract Other			
Grains Hops Yeast Malt Extract Other			
Grains Hops Yeast Malt Extract Other			
Grains Hops Yeast Malt Extract Other			
Grains Hops Yeast Malt Extract Other			
Grains Hops Yeast Malt Extract Other			
Grains Hops Yeast Malt Extract Other			
Grains Hops Yeast Malt Extract Other			
Grains Hops Yeast Malt Extract Other			
Grains Hops Yeast Malt Extract Other			

Brewing Notes

Fermentation Notes

Yeast Pitching Temperature			°F / C
Original Gravity			
Primary Fermentation		days	°F / C
Secondary Fermentation		days	°F / C
Final Gravity			

Bottling Notes   Date

Tasting Notes

Date	Rating	Description

6

Style		Color	SRM
Recipe Type	Malt Extract Partial All Grain	Bitterness	IBU / EBU
Yield		% Alcohol	ABV / ABW
Start Date			

Ingredients

[Circle One]	Amount	Type	Notes
Grains Hops Yeast Malt Extract Other			
Grains Hops Yeast Malt Extract Other			
Grains Hops Yeast Malt Extract Other			
Grains Hops Yeast Malt Extract Other			
Grains Hops Yeast Malt Extract Other			
Grains Hops Yeast Malt Extract Other			
Grains Hops Yeast Malt Extract Other			
Grains Hops Yeast Malt Extract Other			
Grains Hops Yeast Malt Extract Other			
Grains Hops Yeast Malt Extract Other			
Grains Hops Yeast Malt Extract Other			
Grains Hops Yeast Malt Extract Other			
Grains Hops Yeast Malt Extract Other			
Grains Hops Yeast Malt Extract Other			
Grains Hops Yeast Malt Extract Other			
Grains Hops Yeast Malt Extract Other			
Grains Hops Yeast Malt Extract Other			
Grains Hops Yeast Malt Extract Other			

Brewing Notes

Fermentation Notes

Yeast Pitching Temperature		°F / C
Original Gravity		
Primary Fermentation	days	°F / C
Secondary Fermentation	days	°F / C
Final Gravity		

Bottling Notes | Date

Tasting Notes

Date	Rating	Description

7

Style		Color	SRM
Recipe Type	Malt Extract Partial All Grain	Bitterness	IBU / EBU
Yield		% Alcohol	ABV / ABW
Start Date			

Ingredients

[Circle One]	Amount	Type	Notes
Grains Hops Yeast Malt Extract Other			
Grains Hops Yeast Malt Extract Other			
Grains Hops Yeast Malt Extract Other			
Grains Hops Yeast Malt Extract Other			
Grains Hops Yeast Malt Extract Other			
Grains Hops Yeast Malt Extract Other			
Grains Hops Yeast Malt Extract Other			
Grains Hops Yeast Malt Extract Other			
Grains Hops Yeast Malt Extract Other			
Grains Hops Yeast Malt Extract Other			
Grains Hops Yeast Malt Extract Other			
Grains Hops Yeast Malt Extract Other			
Grains Hops Yeast Malt Extract Other			
Grains Hops Yeast Malt Extract Other			
Grains Hops Yeast Malt Extract Other			
Grains Hops Yeast Malt Extract Other			
Grains Hops Yeast Malt Extract Other			
Grains Hops Yeast Malt Extract Other			

Brewing Notes

Fermentation Notes

Yeast Pitching Temperature		°F / C
Original Gravity		
Primary Fermentation	days	°F / C
Secondary Fermentation	days	°F / C
Final Gravity		

Bottling Notes   Date

Tasting Notes

Date	Rating	Description

8

Style		Color	SRM
Recipe Type	Malt Extract Partial All Grain	Bitterness	IBU / EBU
Yield		% Alcohol	ABV / ABW
Start Date			

Ingredients

[Circle One]	Amount	Type	Notes
Grains Hops Yeast Malt Extract Other			
Grains Hops Yeast Malt Extract Other			
Grains Hops Yeast Malt Extract Other			
Grains Hops Yeast Malt Extract Other			
Grains Hops Yeast Malt Extract Other			
Grains Hops Yeast Malt Extract Other			
Grains Hops Yeast Malt Extract Other			
Grains Hops Yeast Malt Extract Other			
Grains Hops Yeast Malt Extract Other			
Grains Hops Yeast Malt Extract Other			
Grains Hops Yeast Malt Extract Other			
Grains Hops Yeast Malt Extract Other			
Grains Hops Yeast Malt Extract Other			
Grains Hops Yeast Malt Extract Other			
Grains Hops Yeast Malt Extract Other			
Grains Hops Yeast Malt Extract Other			
Grains Hops Yeast Malt Extract Other			
Grains Hops Yeast Malt Extract Other			

Brewing Notes

Fermentation Notes

Yeast Pitching Temperature		°F / C
Original Gravity		
Primary Fermentation	days	°F / C
Secondary Fermentation	days	°F / C
Final Gravity		

Bottling Notes

Date

Tasting Notes

Date	Rating	Description

9

Style			Color	SRM
Recipe Type	Malt Extract Partial All Grain		Bitterness	IBU / EBU
Yield			% Alcohol	ABV / ABW
Start Date				

Ingredients

[Circle One]	Amount	Type	Notes
Grains Hops Yeast Malt Extract Other			
Grains Hops Yeast Malt Extract Other			
Grains Hops Yeast Malt Extract Other			
Grains Hops Yeast Malt Extract Other			
Grains Hops Yeast Malt Extract Other			
Grains Hops Yeast Malt Extract Other			
Grains Hops Yeast Malt Extract Other			
Grains Hops Yeast Malt Extract Other			
Grains Hops Yeast Malt Extract Other			
Grains Hops Yeast Malt Extract Other			
Grains Hops Yeast Malt Extract Other			
Grains Hops Yeast Malt Extract Other			
Grains Hops Yeast Malt Extract Other			
Grains Hops Yeast Malt Extract Other			
Grains Hops Yeast Malt Extract Other			
Grains Hops Yeast Malt Extract Other			
Grains Hops Yeast Malt Extract Other			
Grains Hops Yeast Malt Extract Other			

Brewing Notes

Fermentation Notes

Yeast Pitching Temperature		°F / C
Original Gravity		
Primary Fermentation	days	°F / C
Secondary Fermentation	days	°F / C
Final Gravity		

Bottling Notes | Date

Tasting Notes

Date	Rating	Description

10

Style			Color	SRM
Recipe Type	Malt Extract Partial All Grain		Bitterness	IBU / EBU
Yield			% Alcohol	ABV / ABW
Start Date				

Ingredients

[Circle One]	Amount	Type	Notes
Grains Hops Yeast Malt Extract Other			
Grains Hops Yeast Malt Extract Other			
Grains Hops Yeast Malt Extract Other			
Grains Hops Yeast Malt Extract Other			
Grains Hops Yeast Malt Extract Other			
Grains Hops Yeast Malt Extract Other			
Grains Hops Yeast Malt Extract Other			
Grains Hops Yeast Malt Extract Other			
Grains Hops Yeast Malt Extract Other			
Grains Hops Yeast Malt Extract Other			
Grains Hops Yeast Malt Extract Other			
Grains Hops Yeast Malt Extract Other			
Grains Hops Yeast Malt Extract Other			
Grains Hops Yeast Malt Extract Other			
Grains Hops Yeast Malt Extract Other			
Grains Hops Yeast Malt Extract Other			
Grains Hops Yeast Malt Extract Other			
Grains Hops Yeast Malt Extract Other			

Brewing Notes

Fermentation Notes

Yeast Pitching Temperature			°F / C
Original Gravity			
Primary Fermentation		days	°F / C
Secondary Fermentation		days	°F / C
Final Gravity			

Bottling Notes

Date

Tasting Notes

Date	Rating	Description

⧞ II

Style		Color	SRM
Recipe Type	Malt Extract Partial All Grain	**Bitterness**	IBU / EBU
Yield		**% Alcohol**	ABV / ABW
Start Date			

Ingredients

[Circle One]	Amount	Type	Notes
Grains Hops Yeast Malt Extract Other			
Grains Hops Yeast Malt Extract Other			
Grains Hops Yeast Malt Extract Other			
Grains Hops Yeast Malt Extract Other			
Grains Hops Yeast Malt Extract Other			
Grains Hops Yeast Malt Extract Other			
Grains Hops Yeast Malt Extract Other			
Grains Hops Yeast Malt Extract Other			
Grains Hops Yeast Malt Extract Other			
Grains Hops Yeast Malt Extract Other			
Grains Hops Yeast Malt Extract Other			
Grains Hops Yeast Malt Extract Other			
Grains Hops Yeast Malt Extract Other			
Grains Hops Yeast Malt Extract Other			
Grains Hops Yeast Malt Extract Other			
Grains Hops Yeast Malt Extract Other			
Grains Hops Yeast Malt Extract Other			
Grains Hops Yeast Malt Extract Other			

Brewing Notes

Fermentation Notes

Yeast Pitching Temperature			°F / C
Original Gravity			
Primary Fermentation		days	°F / C
Secondary Fermentation		days	°F / C
Final Gravity			

Bottling Notes | Date

Tasting Notes

Date	Rating	Description

12

Style		Color	SRM
Recipe Type	Malt Extract Partial All Grain	Bitterness	IBU / EBU
Yield		% Alcohol	ABV / ABW
Start Date			

Ingredients

[Circle One]	Amount	Type	Notes
Grains Hops Yeast Malt Extract Other			
Grains Hops Yeast Malt Extract Other			
Grains Hops Yeast Malt Extract Other			
Grains Hops Yeast Malt Extract Other			
Grains Hops Yeast Malt Extract Other			
Grains Hops Yeast Malt Extract Other			
Grains Hops Yeast Malt Extract Other			
Grains Hops Yeast Malt Extract Other			
Grains Hops Yeast Malt Extract Other			
Grains Hops Yeast Malt Extract Other			
Grains Hops Yeast Malt Extract Other			
Grains Hops Yeast Malt Extract Other			
Grains Hops Yeast Malt Extract Other			
Grains Hops Yeast Malt Extract Other			
Grains Hops Yeast Malt Extract Other			
Grains Hops Yeast Malt Extract Other			
Grains Hops Yeast Malt Extract Other			
Grains Hops Yeast Malt Extract Other			

Brewing Notes

Fermentation Notes

Yeast Pitching Temperature		°F / C
Original Gravity		
Primary Fermentation	days	°F / C
Secondary Fermentation	days	°F / C
Final Gravity		

Bottling Notes | Date

Tasting Notes

Date	Rating	Description

13

Style				Color	SRM
Recipe Type	Malt Extract	Partial	All Grain	Bitterness	IBU / EBU
Yield				% Alcohol	ABV / ABW
Start Date					

Ingredients

[Circle One]	Amount	Type	Notes
Grains Hops Yeast Malt Extract Other			
Grains Hops Yeast Malt Extract Other			
Grains Hops Yeast Malt Extract Other			
Grains Hops Yeast Malt Extract Other			
Grains Hops Yeast Malt Extract Other			
Grains Hops Yeast Malt Extract Other			
Grains Hops Yeast Malt Extract Other			
Grains Hops Yeast Malt Extract Other			
Grains Hops Yeast Malt Extract Other			
Grains Hops Yeast Malt Extract Other			
Grains Hops Yeast Malt Extract Other			
Grains Hops Yeast Malt Extract Other			
Grains Hops Yeast Malt Extract Other			
Grains Hops Yeast Malt Extract Other			
Grains Hops Yeast Malt Extract Other			
Grains Hops Yeast Malt Extract Other			
Grains Hops Yeast Malt Extract Other			
Grains Hops Yeast Malt Extract Other			

Brewing Notes

Fermentation Notes

Yeast Pitching Temperature		°F / C
Original Gravity		
Primary Fermentation	days	°F / C
Secondary Fermentation	days	°F / C
Final Gravity		

Bottling Notes | Date

Tasting Notes

Date	Rating	Description

14

Style		Color	SRM
Recipe Type	Malt Extract Partial All Grain	Bitterness	IBU / EBU
Yield		% Alcohol	ABV / ABW
Start Date			

Ingredients

[Circle One]	Amount	Type	Notes
Grains Hops Yeast Malt Extract Other			
Grains Hops Yeast Malt Extract Other			
Grains Hops Yeast Malt Extract Other			
Grains Hops Yeast Malt Extract Other			
Grains Hops Yeast Malt Extract Other			
Grains Hops Yeast Malt Extract Other			
Grains Hops Yeast Malt Extract Other			
Grains Hops Yeast Malt Extract Other			
Grains Hops Yeast Malt Extract Other			
Grains Hops Yeast Malt Extract Other			
Grains Hops Yeast Malt Extract Other			
Grains Hops Yeast Malt Extract Other			
Grains Hops Yeast Malt Extract Other			
Grains Hops Yeast Malt Extract Other			
Grains Hops Yeast Malt Extract Other			
Grains Hops Yeast Malt Extract Other			
Grains Hops Yeast Malt Extract Other			
Grains Hops Yeast Malt Extract Other			

Brewing Notes

Fermentation Notes

Yeast Pitching Temperature		°F / C
Original Gravity		
Primary Fermentation	days	°F / C
Secondary Fermentation	days	°F / C
Final Gravity		

Bottling Notes | Date

Tasting Notes

Date	Rating	Description

15

Style		Color	SRM
Recipe Type	Malt Extract Partial All Grain	Bitterness	IBU / EBU
Yield		% Alcohol	ABV / ABW
Start Date			

Ingredients

[Circle One]	Amount	Type	Notes
Grains Hops Yeast Malt Extract Other			
Grains Hops Yeast Malt Extract Other			
Grains Hops Yeast Malt Extract Other			
Grains Hops Yeast Malt Extract Other			
Grains Hops Yeast Malt Extract Other			
Grains Hops Yeast Malt Extract Other			
Grains Hops Yeast Malt Extract Other			
Grains Hops Yeast Malt Extract Other			
Grains Hops Yeast Malt Extract Other			
Grains Hops Yeast Malt Extract Other			
Grains Hops Yeast Malt Extract Other			
Grains Hops Yeast Malt Extract Other			
Grains Hops Yeast Malt Extract Other			
Grains Hops Yeast Malt Extract Other			
Grains Hops Yeast Malt Extract Other			
Grains Hops Yeast Malt Extract Other			
Grains Hops Yeast Malt Extract Other			
Grains Hops Yeast Malt Extract Other			

Brewing Notes

Fermentation Notes

Yeast Pitching Temperature		°F / C
Original Gravity		
Primary Fermentation	days	°F / C
Secondary Fermentation	days	°F / C
Final Gravity		

Bottling Notes	Date

Tasting Notes

Date	Rating	Description

16

Style		Color	SRM
Recipe Type	Malt Extract Partial All Grain	Bitterness	IBU / EBU
Yield		% Alcohol	ABV / ABW
Start Date			

Ingredients

[Circle One]	Amount	Type	Notes
Grains Hops Yeast Malt Extract Other			
Grains Hops Yeast Malt Extract Other			
Grains Hops Yeast Malt Extract Other			
Grains Hops Yeast Malt Extract Other			
Grains Hops Yeast Malt Extract Other			
Grains Hops Yeast Malt Extract Other			
Grains Hops Yeast Malt Extract Other			
Grains Hops Yeast Malt Extract Other			
Grains Hops Yeast Malt Extract Other			
Grains Hops Yeast Malt Extract Other			
Grains Hops Yeast Malt Extract Other			
Grains Hops Yeast Malt Extract Other			
Grains Hops Yeast Malt Extract Other			
Grains Hops Yeast Malt Extract Other			
Grains Hops Yeast Malt Extract Other			
Grains Hops Yeast Malt Extract Other			
Grains Hops Yeast Malt Extract Other			
Grains Hops Yeast Malt Extract Other			

Brewing Notes

Fermentation Notes

Yeast Pitching Temperature		°F / C
Original Gravity		
Primary Fermentation	days	°F / C
Secondary Fermentation	days	°F / C
Final Gravity		

Bottling Notes | Date

Tasting Notes

Date	Rating	Description

17

Style		Color	SRM
Recipe Type	Malt Extract Partial All Grain	Bitterness	IBU / EBU
Yield		% Alcohol	ABV / ABW
Start Date			

Ingredients

[Circle One]	Amount	Type	Notes
Grains Hops Yeast Malt Extract Other			
Grains Hops Yeast Malt Extract Other			
Grains Hops Yeast Malt Extract Other			
Grains Hops Yeast Malt Extract Other			
Grains Hops Yeast Malt Extract Other			
Grains Hops Yeast Malt Extract Other			
Grains Hops Yeast Malt Extract Other			
Grains Hops Yeast Malt Extract Other			
Grains Hops Yeast Malt Extract Other			
Grains Hops Yeast Malt Extract Other			
Grains Hops Yeast Malt Extract Other			
Grains Hops Yeast Malt Extract Other			
Grains Hops Yeast Malt Extract Other			
Grains Hops Yeast Malt Extract Other			
Grains Hops Yeast Malt Extract Other			
Grains Hops Yeast Malt Extract Other			
Grains Hops Yeast Malt Extract Other			
Grains Hops Yeast Malt Extract Other			

Brewing Notes

Fermentation Notes

Yeast Pitching Temperature		°F / C
Original Gravity		
Primary Fermentation	days	°F / C
Secondary Fermentation	days	°F / C
Final Gravity		

Bottling Notes | Date

Tasting Notes

Date	Rating	Description

18

Style		Color	SRM
Recipe Type	Malt Extract Partial All Grain	Bitterness	IBU / EBU
Yield		% Alcohol	ABV / ABW
Start Date			

Ingredients

[Circle One]	Amount	Type	Notes
Grains Hops Yeast Malt Extract Other			
Grains Hops Yeast Malt Extract Other			
Grains Hops Yeast Malt Extract Other			
Grains Hops Yeast Malt Extract Other			
Grains Hops Yeast Malt Extract Other			
Grains Hops Yeast Malt Extract Other			
Grains Hops Yeast Malt Extract Other			
Grains Hops Yeast Malt Extract Other			
Grains Hops Yeast Malt Extract Other			
Grains Hops Yeast Malt Extract Other			
Grains Hops Yeast Malt Extract Other			
Grains Hops Yeast Malt Extract Other			
Grains Hops Yeast Malt Extract Other			
Grains Hops Yeast Malt Extract Other			
Grains Hops Yeast Malt Extract Other			
Grains Hops Yeast Malt Extract Other			
Grains Hops Yeast Malt Extract Other			
Grains Hops Yeast Malt Extract Other			

Brewing Notes

Fermentation Notes

Yeast Pitching Temperature		°F / C
Original Gravity		
Primary Fermentation	days	°F / C
Secondary Fermentation	days	°F / C
Final Gravity		

Bottling Notes | Date

Tasting Notes

Date	Rating	Description

19

Style		Color	SRM
Recipe Type	Malt Extract　Partial　All Grain	Bitterness	IBU / EBU
Yield		% Alcohol	ABV / ABW
Start Date			

Ingredients

[Circle One]	Amount	Type	Notes
Grains　Hops　Yeast Malt Extract　Other			
Grains　Hops　Yeast Malt Extract　Other			
Grains　Hops　Yeast Malt Extract　Other			
Grains　Hops　Yeast Malt Extract　Other			
Grains　Hops　Yeast Malt Extract　Other			
Grains　Hops　Yeast Malt Extract　Other			
Grains　Hops　Yeast Malt Extract　Other			
Grains　Hops　Yeast Malt Extract　Other			
Grains　Hops　Yeast Malt Extract　Other			
Grains　Hops　Yeast Malt Extract　Other			
Grains　Hops　Yeast Malt Extract　Other			
Grains　Hops　Yeast Malt Extract　Other			
Grains　Hops　Yeast Malt Extract　Other			
Grains　Hops　Yeast Malt Extract　Other			
Grains　Hops　Yeast Malt Extract　Other			
Grains　Hops　Yeast Malt Extract　Other			
Grains　Hops　Yeast Malt Extract　Other			
Grains　Hops　Yeast Malt Extract　Other			

Brewing Notes

Fermentation Notes

Yeast Pitching Temperature		°F / C
Original Gravity		
Primary Fermentation	days	°F / C
Secondary Fermentation	days	°F / C
Final Gravity		

Bottling Notes | Date

Tasting Notes

Date	Rating	Description

20

Style		Color	SRM
Recipe Type	Malt Extract Partial All Grain	Bitterness	IBU / EBU
Yield		% Alcohol	ABV / ABW
Start Date			

Ingredients

[Circle One]	Amount	Type	Notes
Grains Hops Yeast Malt Extract Other			
Grains Hops Yeast Malt Extract Other			
Grains Hops Yeast Malt Extract Other			
Grains Hops Yeast Malt Extract Other			
Grains Hops Yeast Malt Extract Other			
Grains Hops Yeast Malt Extract Other			
Grains Hops Yeast Malt Extract Other			
Grains Hops Yeast Malt Extract Other			
Grains Hops Yeast Malt Extract Other			
Grains Hops Yeast Malt Extract Other			
Grains Hops Yeast Malt Extract Other			
Grains Hops Yeast Malt Extract Other			
Grains Hops Yeast Malt Extract Other			
Grains Hops Yeast Malt Extract Other			
Grains Hops Yeast Malt Extract Other			
Grains Hops Yeast Malt Extract Other			
Grains Hops Yeast Malt Extract Other			
Grains Hops Yeast Malt Extract Other			

Brewing Notes

Fermentation Notes

Yeast Pitching Temperature		°F / C
Original Gravity		
Primary Fermentation	days	°F / C
Secondary Fermentation	days	°F / C
Final Gravity		

Bottling Notes

Date

Tasting Notes

Date	Rating	Description

21

Style		Color	SRM
Recipe Type	Malt Extract Partial All Grain	Bitterness	IBU / EBU
Yield		% Alcohol	ABV / ABW
Start Date			

Ingredients

[Circle One]	Amount	Type	Notes
Grains Hops Yeast Malt Extract Other			
Grains Hops Yeast Malt Extract Other			
Grains Hops Yeast Malt Extract Other			
Grains Hops Yeast Malt Extract Other			
Grains Hops Yeast Malt Extract Other			
Grains Hops Yeast Malt Extract Other			
Grains Hops Yeast Malt Extract Other			
Grains Hops Yeast Malt Extract Other			
Grains Hops Yeast Malt Extract Other			
Grains Hops Yeast Malt Extract Other			
Grains Hops Yeast Malt Extract Other			
Grains Hops Yeast Malt Extract Other			
Grains Hops Yeast Malt Extract Other			
Grains Hops Yeast Malt Extract Other			
Grains Hops Yeast Malt Extract Other			
Grains Hops Yeast Malt Extract Other			
Grains Hops Yeast Malt Extract Other			
Grains Hops Yeast Malt Extract Other			

Brewing Notes

Fermentation Notes

Yeast Pitching Temperature			°F / C
Original Gravity			
Primary Fermentation	days		°F / C
Secondary Fermentation	days		°F / C
Final Gravity			

Bottling Notes   Date

Tasting Notes

Date	Rating	Description

22

Style				Color	SRM
Recipe Type	Malt Extract Partial All Grain			Bitterness	IBU / EBU
Yield				% Alcohol	ABV / ABW
Start Date					

Ingredients

[Circle One]	Amount	Type	Notes
Grains Hops Yeast Malt Extract Other			
Grains Hops Yeast Malt Extract Other			
Grains Hops Yeast Malt Extract Other			
Grains Hops Yeast Malt Extract Other			
Grains Hops Yeast Malt Extract Other			
Grains Hops Yeast Malt Extract Other			
Grains Hops Yeast Malt Extract Other			
Grains Hops Yeast Malt Extract Other			
Grains Hops Yeast Malt Extract Other			
Grains Hops Yeast Malt Extract Other			
Grains Hops Yeast Malt Extract Other			
Grains Hops Yeast Malt Extract Other			
Grains Hops Yeast Malt Extract Other			
Grains Hops Yeast Malt Extract Other			
Grains Hops Yeast Malt Extract Other			
Grains Hops Yeast Malt Extract Other			
Grains Hops Yeast Malt Extract Other			
Grains Hops Yeast Malt Extract Other			

Brewing Notes

Fermentation Notes

Yeast Pitching Temperature			°F / C
Original Gravity			
Primary Fermentation	days		°F / C
Secondary Fermentation	days		°F / C
Final Gravity			

Bottling Notes | Date

Tasting Notes

Date	Rating	Description

23

Style		Color	SRM
Recipe Type	Malt Extract Partial All Grain	Bitterness	IBU / EBU
Yield		% Alcohol	ABV / ABW
Start Date			

Ingredients

[Circle One]	Amount	Type	Notes
Grains Hops Yeast Malt Extract Other			
Grains Hops Yeast Malt Extract Other			
Grains Hops Yeast Malt Extract Other			
Grains Hops Yeast Malt Extract Other			
Grains Hops Yeast Malt Extract Other			
Grains Hops Yeast Malt Extract Other			
Grains Hops Yeast Malt Extract Other			
Grains Hops Yeast Malt Extract Other			
Grains Hops Yeast Malt Extract Other			
Grains Hops Yeast Malt Extract Other			
Grains Hops Yeast Malt Extract Other			
Grains Hops Yeast Malt Extract Other			
Grains Hops Yeast Malt Extract Other			
Grains Hops Yeast Malt Extract Other			
Grains Hops Yeast Malt Extract Other			
Grains Hops Yeast Malt Extract Other			
Grains Hops Yeast Malt Extract Other			
Grains Hops Yeast Malt Extract Other			

Brewing Notes

Fermentation Notes

Yeast Pitching Temperature			°F / C
Original Gravity			
Primary Fermentation		days	°F / C
Secondary Fermentation		days	°F / C
Final Gravity			

Bottling Notes   Date

Tasting Notes

Date	Rating	Description

24

Style		Color	SRM
Recipe Type	Malt Extract Partial All Grain	Bitterness	IBU / EBU
Yield		% Alcohol	ABV / ABW
Start Date			

Ingredients

[Circle One]	Amount	Type	Notes
Grains Hops Yeast Malt Extract Other			
Grains Hops Yeast Malt Extract Other			
Grains Hops Yeast Malt Extract Other			
Grains Hops Yeast Malt Extract Other			
Grains Hops Yeast Malt Extract Other			
Grains Hops Yeast Malt Extract Other			
Grains Hops Yeast Malt Extract Other			
Grains Hops Yeast Malt Extract Other			
Grains Hops Yeast Malt Extract Other			
Grains Hops Yeast Malt Extract Other			
Grains Hops Yeast Malt Extract Other			
Grains Hops Yeast Malt Extract Other			
Grains Hops Yeast Malt Extract Other			
Grains Hops Yeast Malt Extract Other			
Grains Hops Yeast Malt Extract Other			
Grains Hops Yeast Malt Extract Other			
Grains Hops Yeast Malt Extract Other			
Grains Hops Yeast Malt Extract Other			

Brewing Notes

Fermentation Notes

Yeast Pitching Temperature		°F / C
Original Gravity		
Primary Fermentation	days	°F / C
Secondary Fermentation	days	°F / C
Final Gravity		

Bottling Notes | Date

Tasting Notes

Date	Rating	Description

25

Style		Color	SRM
Recipe Type	Malt Extract Partial All Grain	Bitterness	IBU / EBU
Yield		% Alcohol	ABV / ABW
Start Date			

Ingredients

[Circle One]	Amount	Type	Notes
Grains Hops Yeast Malt Extract Other			
Grains Hops Yeast Malt Extract Other			
Grains Hops Yeast Malt Extract Other			
Grains Hops Yeast Malt Extract Other			
Grains Hops Yeast Malt Extract Other			
Grains Hops Yeast Malt Extract Other			
Grains Hops Yeast Malt Extract Other			
Grains Hops Yeast Malt Extract Other			
Grains Hops Yeast Malt Extract Other			
Grains Hops Yeast Malt Extract Other			
Grains Hops Yeast Malt Extract Other			
Grains Hops Yeast Malt Extract Other			
Grains Hops Yeast Malt Extract Other			
Grains Hops Yeast Malt Extract Other			
Grains Hops Yeast Malt Extract Other			
Grains Hops Yeast Malt Extract Other			
Grains Hops Yeast Malt Extract Other			
Grains Hops Yeast Malt Extract Other			

Brewing Notes

Fermentation Notes

Yeast Pitching Temperature			°F / C
Original Gravity			
Primary Fermentation	days		°F / C
Secondary Fermentation	days		°F / C
Final Gravity			

Bottling Notes   Date

Tasting Notes

Date	Rating	Description

26

Style		Color	SRM
Recipe Type	Malt Extract Partial All Grain	Bitterness	IBU / EBU
Yield		% Alcohol	ABV / ABW
Start Date			

Ingredients

[Circle One]	Amount	Type	Notes
Grains Hops Yeast Malt Extract Other			
Grains Hops Yeast Malt Extract Other			
Grains Hops Yeast Malt Extract Other			
Grains Hops Yeast Malt Extract Other			
Grains Hops Yeast Malt Extract Other			
Grains Hops Yeast Malt Extract Other			
Grains Hops Yeast Malt Extract Other			
Grains Hops Yeast Malt Extract Other			
Grains Hops Yeast Malt Extract Other			
Grains Hops Yeast Malt Extract Other			
Grains Hops Yeast Malt Extract Other			
Grains Hops Yeast Malt Extract Other			
Grains Hops Yeast Malt Extract Other			
Grains Hops Yeast Malt Extract Other			
Grains Hops Yeast Malt Extract Other			
Grains Hops Yeast Malt Extract Other			
Grains Hops Yeast Malt Extract Other			
Grains Hops Yeast Malt Extract Other			

Brewing Notes

Fermentation Notes

Yeast Pitching Temperature			°F / C
Original Gravity			
Primary Fermentation		days	°F / C
Secondary Fermentation		days	°F / C
Final Gravity			

Bottling Notes   Date

Tasting Notes

Date	Rating	Description

27

Style		Color	SRM
Recipe Type	Malt Extract Partial All Grain	Bitterness	IBU / EBU
Yield		% Alcohol	ABV / ABW
Start Date			

Ingredients

[Circle One]	Amount	Type	Notes
Grains Hops Yeast Malt Extract Other			
Grains Hops Yeast Malt Extract Other			
Grains Hops Yeast Malt Extract Other			
Grains Hops Yeast Malt Extract Other			
Grains Hops Yeast Malt Extract Other			
Grains Hops Yeast Malt Extract Other			
Grains Hops Yeast Malt Extract Other			
Grains Hops Yeast Malt Extract Other			
Grains Hops Yeast Malt Extract Other			
Grains Hops Yeast Malt Extract Other			
Grains Hops Yeast Malt Extract Other			
Grains Hops Yeast Malt Extract Other			
Grains Hops Yeast Malt Extract Other			
Grains Hops Yeast Malt Extract Other			
Grains Hops Yeast Malt Extract Other			
Grains Hops Yeast Malt Extract Other			
Grains Hops Yeast Malt Extract Other			
Grains Hops Yeast Malt Extract Other			

Brewing Notes

Fermentation Notes

Yeast Pitching Temperature		°F / C
Original Gravity		
Primary Fermentation	days	°F / C
Secondary Fermentation	days	°F / C
Final Gravity		

Bottling Notes | Date

Tasting Notes

Date	Rating	Description

28

Style		Color	SRM
Recipe Type	Malt Extract Partial All Grain	Bitterness	IBU / EBU
Yield		% Alcohol	ABV / ABW
Start Date			

Ingredients

[Circle One]	Amount	Type	Notes
Grains Hops Yeast Malt Extract Other			
Grains Hops Yeast Malt Extract Other			
Grains Hops Yeast Malt Extract Other			
Grains Hops Yeast Malt Extract Other			
Grains Hops Yeast Malt Extract Other			
Grains Hops Yeast Malt Extract Other			
Grains Hops Yeast Malt Extract Other			
Grains Hops Yeast Malt Extract Other			
Grains Hops Yeast Malt Extract Other			
Grains Hops Yeast Malt Extract Other			
Grains Hops Yeast Malt Extract Other			
Grains Hops Yeast Malt Extract Other			
Grains Hops Yeast Malt Extract Other			
Grains Hops Yeast Malt Extract Other			
Grains Hops Yeast Malt Extract Other			
Grains Hops Yeast Malt Extract Other			
Grains Hops Yeast Malt Extract Other			
Grains Hops Yeast Malt Extract Other			

Brewing Notes

Fermentation Notes

Yeast Pitching Temperature			°F / C
Original Gravity			
Primary Fermentation	days		°F / C
Secondary Fermentation	days		°F / C
Final Gravity			

Bottling Notes | Date

Tasting Notes

Date	Rating	Description

29

Style				Color	SRM
Recipe Type	Malt Extract	Partial	All Grain	Bitterness	IBU / EBU
Yield				% Alcohol	ABV / ABW
Start Date					

Ingredients

[Circle One]	Amount	Type	Notes
Grains Hops Yeast Malt Extract Other			
Grains Hops Yeast Malt Extract Other			
Grains Hops Yeast Malt Extract Other			
Grains Hops Yeast Malt Extract Other			
Grains Hops Yeast Malt Extract Other			
Grains Hops Yeast Malt Extract Other			
Grains Hops Yeast Malt Extract Other			
Grains Hops Yeast Malt Extract Other			
Grains Hops Yeast Malt Extract Other			
Grains Hops Yeast Malt Extract Other			
Grains Hops Yeast Malt Extract Other			
Grains Hops Yeast Malt Extract Other			
Grains Hops Yeast Malt Extract Other			
Grains Hops Yeast Malt Extract Other			
Grains Hops Yeast Malt Extract Other			
Grains Hops Yeast Malt Extract Other			
Grains Hops Yeast Malt Extract Other			
Grains Hops Yeast Malt Extract Other			
Grains Hops Yeast Malt Extract Other			

Brewing Notes

Fermentation Notes

Yeast Pitching Temperature		°F / C
Original Gravity		
Primary Fermentation	days	°F / C
Secondary Fermentation	days	°F / C
Final Gravity		

Bottling Notes | Date

Tasting Notes

Date	Rating	Description

30

Style		Color	SRM
Recipe Type	Malt Extract Partial All Grain	Bitterness	IBU / EBU
Yield		% Alcohol	ABV / ABW
Start Date			

Ingredients

[Circle One]	Amount	Type	Notes
Grains Hops Yeast Malt Extract Other			
Grains Hops Yeast Malt Extract Other			
Grains Hops Yeast Malt Extract Other			
Grains Hops Yeast Malt Extract Other			
Grains Hops Yeast Malt Extract Other			
Grains Hops Yeast Malt Extract Other			
Grains Hops Yeast Malt Extract Other			
Grains Hops Yeast Malt Extract Other			
Grains Hops Yeast Malt Extract Other			
Grains Hops Yeast Malt Extract Other			
Grains Hops Yeast Malt Extract Other			
Grains Hops Yeast Malt Extract Other			
Grains Hops Yeast Malt Extract Other			
Grains Hops Yeast Malt Extract Other			
Grains Hops Yeast Malt Extract Other			
Grains Hops Yeast Malt Extract Other			
Grains Hops Yeast Malt Extract Other			
Grains Hops Yeast Malt Extract Other			

Brewing Notes

Fermentation Notes

Yeast Pitching Temperature		°F / C
Original Gravity		
Primary Fermentation	days	°F / C
Secondary Fermentation	days	°F / C
Final Gravity		

Bottling Notes   Date

Tasting Notes

Date	Rating	Description

31

Style		Color	SRM
Recipe Type	Malt Extract Partial All Grain	Bitterness	IBU / EBU
Yield		% Alcohol	ABV / ABW
Start Date			

Ingredients

[Circle One]	Amount	Type	Notes
Grains Hops Yeast Malt Extract Other			
Grains Hops Yeast Malt Extract Other			
Grains Hops Yeast Malt Extract Other			
Grains Hops Yeast Malt Extract Other			
Grains Hops Yeast Malt Extract Other			
Grains Hops Yeast Malt Extract Other			
Grains Hops Yeast Malt Extract Other			
Grains Hops Yeast Malt Extract Other			
Grains Hops Yeast Malt Extract Other			
Grains Hops Yeast Malt Extract Other			
Grains Hops Yeast Malt Extract Other			
Grains Hops Yeast Malt Extract Other			
Grains Hops Yeast Malt Extract Other			
Grains Hops Yeast Malt Extract Other			
Grains Hops Yeast Malt Extract Other			
Grains Hops Yeast Malt Extract Other			
Grains Hops Yeast Malt Extract Other			
Grains Hops Yeast Malt Extract Other			
Grains Hops Yeast Malt Extract Other			

Brewing Notes

Fermentation Notes

Yeast Pitching Temperature		°F / C
Original Gravity		
Primary Fermentation	days	°F / C
Secondary Fermentation	days	°F / C
Final Gravity		

Bottling Notes

Date

Tasting Notes

Date	Rating	Description

32

Style			Color	SRM
Recipe Type	Malt Extract Partial All Grain		Bitterness	IBU / EBU
Yield			% Alcohol	ABV / ABW
Start Date				

Ingredients

[Circle One]	Amount	Type	Notes
Grains Hops Yeast Malt Extract Other			
Grains Hops Yeast Malt Extract Other			
Grains Hops Yeast Malt Extract Other			
Grains Hops Yeast Malt Extract Other			
Grains Hops Yeast Malt Extract Other			
Grains Hops Yeast Malt Extract Other			
Grains Hops Yeast Malt Extract Other			
Grains Hops Yeast Malt Extract Other			
Grains Hops Yeast Malt Extract Other			
Grains Hops Yeast Malt Extract Other			
Grains Hops Yeast Malt Extract Other			
Grains Hops Yeast Malt Extract Other			
Grains Hops Yeast Malt Extract Other			
Grains Hops Yeast Malt Extract Other			
Grains Hops Yeast Malt Extract Other			
Grains Hops Yeast Malt Extract Other			
Grains Hops Yeast Malt Extract Other			
Grains Hops Yeast Malt Extract Other			

Brewing Notes

Fermentation Notes

Yeast Pitching Temperature		°F / C
Original Gravity		
Primary Fermentation	days	°F / C
Secondary Fermentation	days	°F / C
Final Gravity		

Bottling Notes   Date

Tasting Notes

Date	Rating	Description

33

Style		Color	SRM
Recipe Type	Malt Extract Partial All Grain	Bitterness	IBU / EBU
Yield		% Alcohol	ABV / ABW
Start Date			

Ingredients

[Circle One]	Amount	Type	Notes
Grains Hops Yeast Malt Extract Other			
Grains Hops Yeast Malt Extract Other			
Grains Hops Yeast Malt Extract Other			
Grains Hops Yeast Malt Extract Other			
Grains Hops Yeast Malt Extract Other			
Grains Hops Yeast Malt Extract Other			
Grains Hops Yeast Malt Extract Other			
Grains Hops Yeast Malt Extract Other			
Grains Hops Yeast Malt Extract Other			
Grains Hops Yeast Malt Extract Other			
Grains Hops Yeast Malt Extract Other			
Grains Hops Yeast Malt Extract Other			
Grains Hops Yeast Malt Extract Other			
Grains Hops Yeast Malt Extract Other			
Grains Hops Yeast Malt Extract Other			
Grains Hops Yeast Malt Extract Other			
Grains Hops Yeast Malt Extract Other			
Grains Hops Yeast Malt Extract Other			

Brewing Notes

Fermentation Notes

Yeast Pitching Temperature		°F / C
Original Gravity		
Primary Fermentation	days	°F / C
Secondary Fermentation	days	°F / C
Final Gravity		

Bottling Notes

Date

Tasting Notes

Date	Rating	Description

34

Style		Color	SRM
Recipe Type	Malt Extract Partial All Grain	Bitterness	IBU / EBU
Yield		% Alcohol	ABV / ABW
Start Date			

Ingredients

[Circle One]	Amount	Type	Notes
Grains Hops Yeast Malt Extract Other			
Grains Hops Yeast Malt Extract Other			
Grains Hops Yeast Malt Extract Other			
Grains Hops Yeast Malt Extract Other			
Grains Hops Yeast Malt Extract Other			
Grains Hops Yeast Malt Extract Other			
Grains Hops Yeast Malt Extract Other			
Grains Hops Yeast Malt Extract Other			
Grains Hops Yeast Malt Extract Other			
Grains Hops Yeast Malt Extract Other			
Grains Hops Yeast Malt Extract Other			
Grains Hops Yeast Malt Extract Other			
Grains Hops Yeast Malt Extract Other			
Grains Hops Yeast Malt Extract Other			
Grains Hops Yeast Malt Extract Other			
Grains Hops Yeast Malt Extract Other			
Grains Hops Yeast Malt Extract Other			
Grains Hops Yeast Malt Extract Other			

Brewing Notes

Fermentation Notes

Yeast Pitching Temperature		°F / C
Original Gravity		
Primary Fermentation	days	°F / C
Secondary Fermentation	days	°F / C
Final Gravity		

Bottling Notes | Date

Tasting Notes

Date	Rating	Description

35

Style		Color	SRM
Recipe Type	Malt Extract Partial All Grain	Bitterness	IBU / EBU
Yield		% Alcohol	ABV / ABW
Start Date			

Ingredients

[Circle One]	Amount	Type	Notes
Grains Hops Yeast Malt Extract Other			
Grains Hops Yeast Malt Extract Other			
Grains Hops Yeast Malt Extract Other			
Grains Hops Yeast Malt Extract Other			
Grains Hops Yeast Malt Extract Other			
Grains Hops Yeast Malt Extract Other			
Grains Hops Yeast Malt Extract Other			
Grains Hops Yeast Malt Extract Other			
Grains Hops Yeast Malt Extract Other			
Grains Hops Yeast Malt Extract Other			
Grains Hops Yeast Malt Extract Other			
Grains Hops Yeast Malt Extract Other			
Grains Hops Yeast Malt Extract Other			
Grains Hops Yeast Malt Extract Other			
Grains Hops Yeast Malt Extract Other			
Grains Hops Yeast Malt Extract Other			
Grains Hops Yeast Malt Extract Other			
Grains Hops Yeast Malt Extract Other			

Brewing Notes

Fermentation Notes

Yeast Pitching Temperature			°F / C
Original Gravity			
Primary Fermentation		days	°F / C
Secondary Fermentation		days	°F / C
Final Gravity			

Bottling Notes

Date

Tasting Notes

Date	Rating	Description

36

Style		Color	SRM
Recipe Type	Malt Extract Partial All Grain	Bitterness	IBU / EBU
Yield		% Alcohol	ABV / ABW
Start Date			

Ingredients

[Circle One]	Amount	Type	Notes
Grains Hops Yeast Malt Extract Other			
Grains Hops Yeast Malt Extract Other			
Grains Hops Yeast Malt Extract Other			
Grains Hops Yeast Malt Extract Other			
Grains Hops Yeast Malt Extract Other			
Grains Hops Yeast Malt Extract Other			
Grains Hops Yeast Malt Extract Other			
Grains Hops Yeast Malt Extract Other			
Grains Hops Yeast Malt Extract Other			
Grains Hops Yeast Malt Extract Other			
Grains Hops Yeast Malt Extract Other			
Grains Hops Yeast Malt Extract Other			
Grains Hops Yeast Malt Extract Other			
Grains Hops Yeast Malt Extract Other			
Grains Hops Yeast Malt Extract Other			
Grains Hops Yeast Malt Extract Other			
Grains Hops Yeast Malt Extract Other			
Grains Hops Yeast Malt Extract Other			

Brewing Notes

Fermentation Notes

Yeast Pitching Temperature		°F / C
Original Gravity		
Primary Fermentation	days	°F / C
Secondary Fermentation	days	°F / C
Final Gravity		

Bottling Notes | Date

Tasting Notes

Date	Rating	Description

Style		Color	SRM
Recipe Type	Malt Extract Partial All Grain	Bitterness	IBU / EBU
Yield		% Alcohol	ABV / ABW
Start Date			

Ingredients

[Circle One]	Amount	Type	Notes
Grains Hops Yeast Malt Extract Other			
Grains Hops Yeast Malt Extract Other			
Grains Hops Yeast Malt Extract Other			
Grains Hops Yeast Malt Extract Other			
Grains Hops Yeast Malt Extract Other			
Grains Hops Yeast Malt Extract Other			
Grains Hops Yeast Malt Extract Other			
Grains Hops Yeast Malt Extract Other			
Grains Hops Yeast Malt Extract Other			
Grains Hops Yeast Malt Extract Other			
Grains Hops Yeast Malt Extract Other			
Grains Hops Yeast Malt Extract Other			
Grains Hops Yeast Malt Extract Other			
Grains Hops Yeast Malt Extract Other			
Grains Hops Yeast Malt Extract Other			
Grains Hops Yeast Malt Extract Other			
Grains Hops Yeast Malt Extract Other			
Grains Hops Yeast Malt Extract Other			

Brewing Notes

Fermentation Notes

Yeast Pitching Temperature		°F / C
Original Gravity		
Primary Fermentation	days	°F / C
Secondary Fermentation	days	°F / C
Final Gravity		

Bottling Notes | Date

Tasting Notes

Date	Rating	Description

38

Style		Color	SRM
Recipe Type	Malt Extract Partial All Grain	Bitterness	IBU / EBU
Yield		% Alcohol	ABV / ABW
Start Date			

Ingredients

[Circle One]	Amount	Type	Notes
Grains Hops Yeast Malt Extract Other			
Grains Hops Yeast Malt Extract Other			
Grains Hops Yeast Malt Extract Other			
Grains Hops Yeast Malt Extract Other			
Grains Hops Yeast Malt Extract Other			
Grains Hops Yeast Malt Extract Other			
Grains Hops Yeast Malt Extract Other			
Grains Hops Yeast Malt Extract Other			
Grains Hops Yeast Malt Extract Other			
Grains Hops Yeast Malt Extract Other			
Grains Hops Yeast Malt Extract Other			
Grains Hops Yeast Malt Extract Other			
Grains Hops Yeast Malt Extract Other			
Grains Hops Yeast Malt Extract Other			
Grains Hops Yeast Malt Extract Other			
Grains Hops Yeast Malt Extract Other			
Grains Hops Yeast Malt Extract Other			
Grains Hops Yeast Malt Extract Other			

Brewing Notes

Fermentation Notes

Yeast Pitching Temperature			°F / C
Original Gravity			
Primary Fermentation	days		°F / C
Secondary Fermentation	days		°F / C
Final Gravity			

Bottling Notes | Date

Tasting Notes

Date	Rating	Description

39

Style		Color	SRM
Recipe Type	Malt Extract Partial All Grain	Bitterness	IBU / EBU
Yield		% Alcohol	ABV / ABW
Start Date			

Ingredients

[Circle One]	Amount	Type	Notes
Grains Hops Yeast Malt Extract Other			
Grains Hops Yeast Malt Extract Other			
Grains Hops Yeast Malt Extract Other			
Grains Hops Yeast Malt Extract Other			
Grains Hops Yeast Malt Extract Other			
Grains Hops Yeast Malt Extract Other			
Grains Hops Yeast Malt Extract Other			
Grains Hops Yeast Malt Extract Other			
Grains Hops Yeast Malt Extract Other			
Grains Hops Yeast Malt Extract Other			
Grains Hops Yeast Malt Extract Other			
Grains Hops Yeast Malt Extract Other			
Grains Hops Yeast Malt Extract Other			
Grains Hops Yeast Malt Extract Other			
Grains Hops Yeast Malt Extract Other			
Grains Hops Yeast Malt Extract Other			
Grains Hops Yeast Malt Extract Other			
Grains Hops Yeast Malt Extract Other			

Brewing Notes

Fermentation Notes

Yeast Pitching Temperature		°F / C
Original Gravity		
Primary Fermentation	days	°F / C
Secondary Fermentation	days	°F / C
Final Gravity		

Bottling Notes   Date

Tasting Notes

Date	Rating	Description

40

Style		Color	SRM
Recipe Type	Malt Extract Partial All Grain	Bitterness	IBU / EBU
Yield		% Alcohol	ABV / ABW
Start Date			

Ingredients

[Circle One]	Amount	Type	Notes
Grains Hops Yeast Malt Extract Other			
Grains Hops Yeast Malt Extract Other			
Grains Hops Yeast Malt Extract Other			
Grains Hops Yeast Malt Extract Other			
Grains Hops Yeast Malt Extract Other			
Grains Hops Yeast Malt Extract Other			
Grains Hops Yeast Malt Extract Other			
Grains Hops Yeast Malt Extract Other			
Grains Hops Yeast Malt Extract Other			
Grains Hops Yeast Malt Extract Other			
Grains Hops Yeast Malt Extract Other			
Grains Hops Yeast Malt Extract Other			
Grains Hops Yeast Malt Extract Other			
Grains Hops Yeast Malt Extract Other			
Grains Hops Yeast Malt Extract Other			
Grains Hops Yeast Malt Extract Other			
Grains Hops Yeast Malt Extract Other			
Grains Hops Yeast Malt Extract Other			

Brewing Notes

Fermentation Notes

Yeast Pitching Temperature		°F / C
Original Gravity		
Primary Fermentation	days	°F / C
Secondary Fermentation	days	°F / C
Final Gravity		

Bottling Notes   Date

Tasting Notes

Date	Rating	Description

41

Style				Color	SRM
Recipe Type	Malt Extract	Partial	All Grain	Bitterness	IBU / EBU
Yield				% Alcohol	ABV / ABW
Start Date					

Ingredients

[Circle One]	Amount	Type	Notes
Grains Hops Yeast Malt Extract Other			
Grains Hops Yeast Malt Extract Other			
Grains Hops Yeast Malt Extract Other			
Grains Hops Yeast Malt Extract Other			
Grains Hops Yeast Malt Extract Other			
Grains Hops Yeast Malt Extract Other			
Grains Hops Yeast Malt Extract Other			
Grains Hops Yeast Malt Extract Other			
Grains Hops Yeast Malt Extract Other			
Grains Hops Yeast Malt Extract Other			
Grains Hops Yeast Malt Extract Other			
Grains Hops Yeast Malt Extract Other			
Grains Hops Yeast Malt Extract Other			
Grains Hops Yeast Malt Extract Other			
Grains Hops Yeast Malt Extract Other			
Grains Hops Yeast Malt Extract Other			
Grains Hops Yeast Malt Extract Other			
Grains Hops Yeast Malt Extract Other			

Brewing Notes

Fermentation Notes

Yeast Pitching Temperature		°F / C
Original Gravity		
Primary Fermentation	days	°F / C
Secondary Fermentation	days	°F / C
Final Gravity		

Bottling Notes   Date

Tasting Notes

Date	Rating	Description

42

Style		Color	SRM
Recipe Type	Malt Extract Partial All Grain	Bitterness	IBU / EBU
Yield		% Alcohol	ABV / ABW
Start Date			

Ingredients

[Circle One]	Amount	Type	Notes
Grains Hops Yeast Malt Extract Other			
Grains Hops Yeast Malt Extract Other			
Grains Hops Yeast Malt Extract Other			
Grains Hops Yeast Malt Extract Other			
Grains Hops Yeast Malt Extract Other			
Grains Hops Yeast Malt Extract Other			
Grains Hops Yeast Malt Extract Other			
Grains Hops Yeast Malt Extract Other			
Grains Hops Yeast Malt Extract Other			
Grains Hops Yeast Malt Extract Other			
Grains Hops Yeast Malt Extract Other			
Grains Hops Yeast Malt Extract Other			
Grains Hops Yeast Malt Extract Other			
Grains Hops Yeast Malt Extract Other			
Grains Hops Yeast Malt Extract Other			
Grains Hops Yeast Malt Extract Other			
Grains Hops Yeast Malt Extract Other			
Grains Hops Yeast Malt Extract Other			

Brewing Notes

Fermentation Notes

Yeast Pitching Temperature			°F / C
Original Gravity			
Primary Fermentation	days		°F / C
Secondary Fermentation	days		°F / C
Final Gravity			

Bottling Notes   Date

Tasting Notes

Date	Rating	Description

43

Style		Color	SRM
Recipe Type	Malt Extract Partial All Grain	Bitterness	IBU / EBU
Yield		% Alcohol	ABV / ABW
Start Date			

Ingredients

[Circle One]	Amount	Type	Notes
Grains Hops Yeast Malt Extract Other			
Grains Hops Yeast Malt Extract Other			
Grains Hops Yeast Malt Extract Other			
Grains Hops Yeast Malt Extract Other			
Grains Hops Yeast Malt Extract Other			
Grains Hops Yeast Malt Extract Other			
Grains Hops Yeast Malt Extract Other			
Grains Hops Yeast Malt Extract Other			
Grains Hops Yeast Malt Extract Other			
Grains Hops Yeast Malt Extract Other			
Grains Hops Yeast Malt Extract Other			
Grains Hops Yeast Malt Extract Other			
Grains Hops Yeast Malt Extract Other			
Grains Hops Yeast Malt Extract Other			
Grains Hops Yeast Malt Extract Other			
Grains Hops Yeast Malt Extract Other			
Grains Hops Yeast Malt Extract Other			
Grains Hops Yeast Malt Extract Other			

Brewing Notes

Fermentation Notes

Yeast Pitching Temperature		°F / C
Original Gravity		
Primary Fermentation	days	°F / C
Secondary Fermentation	days	°F / C
Final Gravity		

Bottling Notes | Date

Tasting Notes

Date	Rating	Description

44

Style		Color	SRM
Recipe Type	Malt Extract Partial All Grain	Bitterness	IBU / EBU
Yield		% Alcohol	ABV / ABW
Start Date			

Ingredients

[Circle One]	Amount	Type	Notes
Grains Hops Yeast Malt Extract Other			
Grains Hops Yeast Malt Extract Other			
Grains Hops Yeast Malt Extract Other			
Grains Hops Yeast Malt Extract Other			
Grains Hops Yeast Malt Extract Other			
Grains Hops Yeast Malt Extract Other			
Grains Hops Yeast Malt Extract Other			
Grains Hops Yeast Malt Extract Other			
Grains Hops Yeast Malt Extract Other			
Grains Hops Yeast Malt Extract Other			
Grains Hops Yeast Malt Extract Other			
Grains Hops Yeast Malt Extract Other			
Grains Hops Yeast Malt Extract Other			
Grains Hops Yeast Malt Extract Other			
Grains Hops Yeast Malt Extract Other			
Grains Hops Yeast Malt Extract Other			
Grains Hops Yeast Malt Extract Other			
Grains Hops Yeast Malt Extract Other			

Brewing Notes

Fermentation Notes

Yeast Pitching Temperature		°F / C
Original Gravity		
Primary Fermentation	days	°F / C
Secondary Fermentation	days	°F / C
Final Gravity		

Bottling Notes   Date

Tasting Notes

Date	Rating	Description

45

Style		Color	SRM
Recipe Type	Malt Extract Partial All Grain	Bitterness	IBU / EBU
Yield		% Alcohol	ABV / ABW
Start Date			

Ingredients

[Circle One]	Amount	Type	Notes
Grains Hops Yeast Malt Extract Other			
Grains Hops Yeast Malt Extract Other			
Grains Hops Yeast Malt Extract Other			
Grains Hops Yeast Malt Extract Other			
Grains Hops Yeast Malt Extract Other			
Grains Hops Yeast Malt Extract Other			
Grains Hops Yeast Malt Extract Other			
Grains Hops Yeast Malt Extract Other			
Grains Hops Yeast Malt Extract Other			
Grains Hops Yeast Malt Extract Other			
Grains Hops Yeast Malt Extract Other			
Grains Hops Yeast Malt Extract Other			
Grains Hops Yeast Malt Extract Other			
Grains Hops Yeast Malt Extract Other			
Grains Hops Yeast Malt Extract Other			
Grains Hops Yeast Malt Extract Other			
Grains Hops Yeast Malt Extract Other			
Grains Hops Yeast Malt Extract Other			

Brewing Notes

Fermentation Notes

Yeast Pitching Temperature		°F / C
Original Gravity		
Primary Fermentation	days	°F / C
Secondary Fermentation	days	°F / C
Final Gravity		

Bottling Notes

Date

Tasting Notes

Date	Rating	Description

46

Style		Color	SRM
Recipe Type	Malt Extract Partial All Grain	Bitterness	IBU / EBU
Yield		% Alcohol	ABV / ABW
Start Date			

Ingredients

[Circle One]	Amount	Type	Notes
Grains Hops Yeast Malt Extract Other			
Grains Hops Yeast Malt Extract Other			
Grains Hops Yeast Malt Extract Other			
Grains Hops Yeast Malt Extract Other			
Grains Hops Yeast Malt Extract Other			
Grains Hops Yeast Malt Extract Other			
Grains Hops Yeast Malt Extract Other			
Grains Hops Yeast Malt Extract Other			
Grains Hops Yeast Malt Extract Other			
Grains Hops Yeast Malt Extract Other			
Grains Hops Yeast Malt Extract Other			
Grains Hops Yeast Malt Extract Other			
Grains Hops Yeast Malt Extract Other			
Grains Hops Yeast Malt Extract Other			
Grains Hops Yeast Malt Extract Other			
Grains Hops Yeast Malt Extract Other			
Grains Hops Yeast Malt Extract Other			

Brewing Notes

Fermentation Notes

Yeast Pitching Temperature			°F / C
Original Gravity			
Primary Fermentation		days	°F / C
Secondary Fermentation		days	°F / C
Final Gravity			

Bottling Notes

Date

Tasting Notes

Date	Rating	Description

47

Style		Color	SRM
Recipe Type	Malt Extract Partial All Grain	Bitterness	IBU / EBU
Yield		% Alcohol	ABV / ABW
Start Date			

Ingredients

[Circle One]	Amount	Type	Notes
Grains Hops Yeast Malt Extract Other			
Grains Hops Yeast Malt Extract Other			
Grains Hops Yeast Malt Extract Other			
Grains Hops Yeast Malt Extract Other			
Grains Hops Yeast Malt Extract Other			
Grains Hops Yeast Malt Extract Other			
Grains Hops Yeast Malt Extract Other			
Grains Hops Yeast Malt Extract Other			
Grains Hops Yeast Malt Extract Other			
Grains Hops Yeast Malt Extract Other			
Grains Hops Yeast Malt Extract Other			
Grains Hops Yeast Malt Extract Other			
Grains Hops Yeast Malt Extract Other			
Grains Hops Yeast Malt Extract Other			
Grains Hops Yeast Malt Extract Other			
Grains Hops Yeast Malt Extract Other			
Grains Hops Yeast Malt Extract Other			
Grains Hops Yeast Malt Extract Other			

Brewing Notes

Fermentation Notes

Yeast Pitching Temperature		°F / C
Original Gravity		
Primary Fermentation	days	°F / C
Secondary Fermentation	days	°F / C
Final Gravity		

Bottling Notes | Date

Tasting Notes

Date	Rating	Description

48

Style		Color	SRM
Recipe Type	Malt Extract Partial All Grain	Bitterness	IBU / EBU
Yield		% Alcohol	ABV / ABW
Start Date			

Ingredients

[Circle One]	Amount	Type	Notes
Grains Hops Yeast Malt Extract Other			
Grains Hops Yeast Malt Extract Other			
Grains Hops Yeast Malt Extract Other			
Grains Hops Yeast Malt Extract Other			
Grains Hops Yeast Malt Extract Other			
Grains Hops Yeast Malt Extract Other			
Grains Hops Yeast Malt Extract Other			
Grains Hops Yeast Malt Extract Other			
Grains Hops Yeast Malt Extract Other			
Grains Hops Yeast Malt Extract Other			
Grains Hops Yeast Malt Extract Other			
Grains Hops Yeast Malt Extract Other			
Grains Hops Yeast Malt Extract Other			
Grains Hops Yeast Malt Extract Other			
Grains Hops Yeast Malt Extract Other			
Grains Hops Yeast Malt Extract Other			
Grains Hops Yeast Malt Extract Other			
Grains Hops Yeast Malt Extract Other			

Brewing Notes

Fermentation Notes

Yeast Pitching Temperature			°F / C
Original Gravity			
Primary Fermentation	days		°F / C
Secondary Fermentation	days		°F / C
Final Gravity			

Bottling Notes | Date

Tasting Notes

Date	Rating	Description

49

Style		Color	SRM
Recipe Type	Malt Extract Partial All Grain	Bitterness	IBU / EBU
Yield		% Alcohol	ABV / ABW
Start Date			

Ingredients

[Circle One]	Amount	Type	Notes
Grains Hops Yeast Malt Extract Other			
Grains Hops Yeast Malt Extract Other			
Grains Hops Yeast Malt Extract Other			
Grains Hops Yeast Malt Extract Other			
Grains Hops Yeast Malt Extract Other			
Grains Hops Yeast Malt Extract Other			
Grains Hops Yeast Malt Extract Other			
Grains Hops Yeast Malt Extract Other			
Grains Hops Yeast Malt Extract Other			
Grains Hops Yeast Malt Extract Other			
Grains Hops Yeast Malt Extract Other			
Grains Hops Yeast Malt Extract Other			
Grains Hops Yeast Malt Extract Other			
Grains Hops Yeast Malt Extract Other			
Grains Hops Yeast Malt Extract Other			
Grains Hops Yeast Malt Extract Other			
Grains Hops Yeast Malt Extract Other			
Grains Hops Yeast Malt Extract Other			

Brewing Notes

Fermentation Notes

Yeast Pitching Temperature		°F / C
Original Gravity		
Primary Fermentation	days	°F / C
Secondary Fermentation	days	°F / C
Final Gravity		

Bottling Notes | Date

Tasting Notes

Date	Rating	Description

50

Style		Color	SRM
Recipe Type	Malt Extract Partial All Grain	Bitterness	IBU / EBU
Yield		% Alcohol	ABV / ABW
Start Date			

Ingredients

[Circle One]	Amount	Type	Notes
Grains Hops Yeast Malt Extract Other			
Grains Hops Yeast Malt Extract Other			
Grains Hops Yeast Malt Extract Other			
Grains Hops Yeast Malt Extract Other			
Grains Hops Yeast Malt Extract Other			
Grains Hops Yeast Malt Extract Other			
Grains Hops Yeast Malt Extract Other			
Grains Hops Yeast Malt Extract Other			
Grains Hops Yeast Malt Extract Other			
Grains Hops Yeast Malt Extract Other			
Grains Hops Yeast Malt Extract Other			
Grains Hops Yeast Malt Extract Other			
Grains Hops Yeast Malt Extract Other			
Grains Hops Yeast Malt Extract Other			
Grains Hops Yeast Malt Extract Other			
Grains Hops Yeast Malt Extract Other			
Grains Hops Yeast Malt Extract Other			
Grains Hops Yeast Malt Extract Other			

Brewing Notes

Fermentation Notes

Yeast Pitching Temperature		°F / C
Original Gravity		
Primary Fermentation	days	°F / C
Secondary Fermentation	days	°F / C
Final Gravity		

Bottling Notes | Date

Tasting Notes

Date	Rating	Description

REFERENCES + NOTES

Common Conversions

Temperature

$°F = °C \times 9/5 + 32$

$°C = (°F - 32) \times 5/9$

Weight

1 oz = 28.349 g

1 kg = 2.2 lbs

1.5 kg = 3.3 lbs

Volume

1 US gal = 0.8 Imperial gal

1 US gal = 3.785 L

1 US gal = 128 oz

Brewing

$ABV = (OG - FG) \times 131$

$ABW = (OG - FG) \times 1.05$

$ABV = ABW \times 1.25$

$ABW = ABV \times 0.8$

Bottling

1 US gal = ~ 10.5 12 oz bottles

1 US gal = ~ 6 22 oz bottles

1 US gal = ~ 7.5 0.5 L bottles

1 US gal = ~ 3.5 1 L bottles

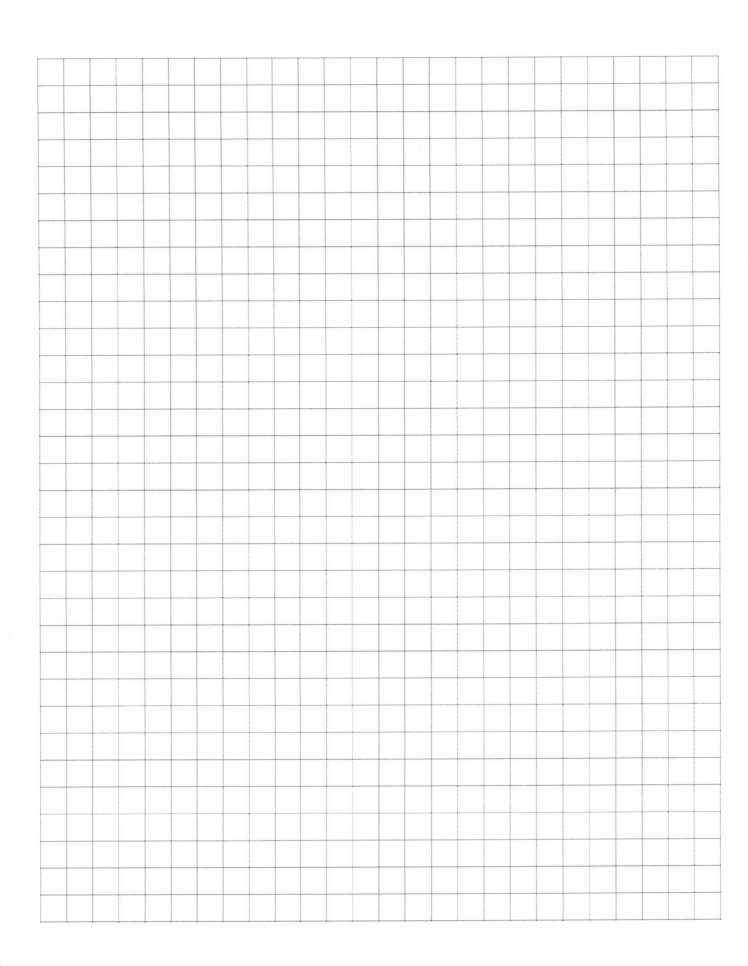

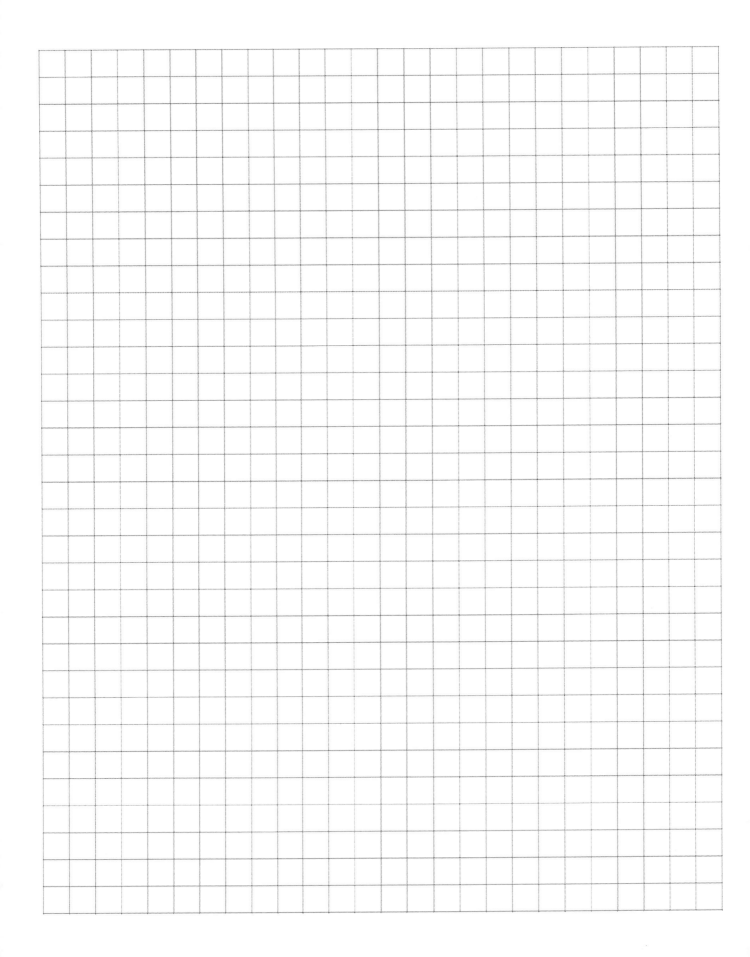

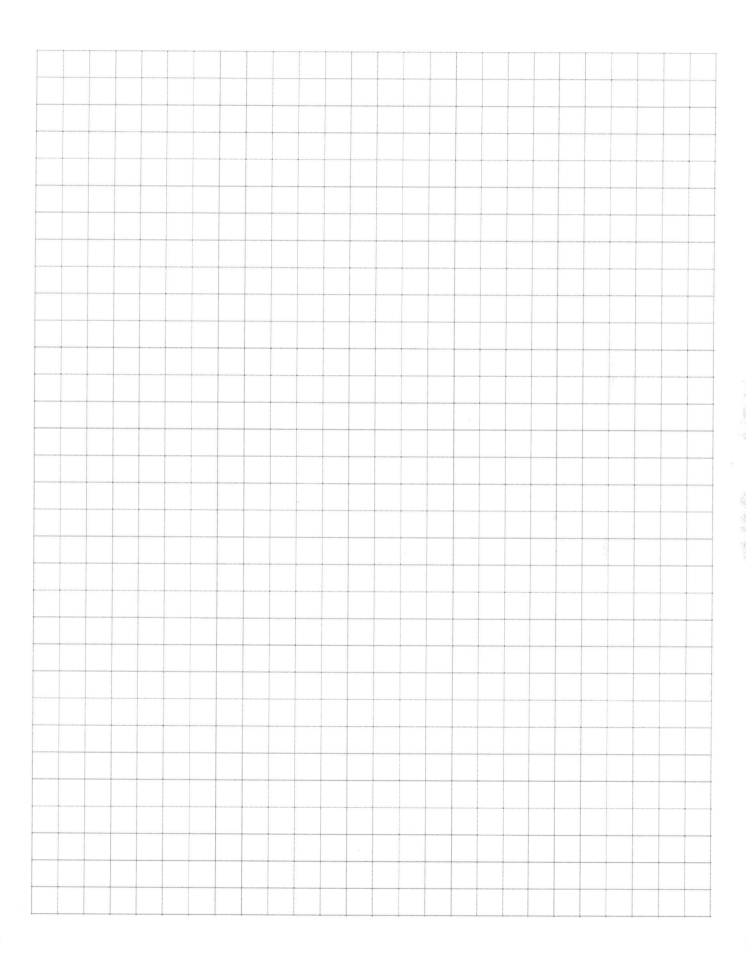

Made in the USA
Lexington, KY
13 December 2015